PORTRAIT OF
WIMBLEDON

Beata Moore

HALSGROVE

First published in Great Britain in 2012

Copyright © Beata Moore 2012

British Library Cataloguing-in-Publication Data
A CIP record for this title is available from the British Library

ISBN 978 0 85704 130 2

HALSGROVE
Halsgrove House,
Ryelands Business Park,
Bagley Road, Wellington, Somerset TA21 9PZ
Tel: 01823 653777   Fax: 01823 216796
email: sales@halsgrove.com

Part of the Halsgrove group of companies.
Information on all Halsgrove titles is available at:
www.halsgrove.com

Printed in China by Everbest Printing Co Ltd

CONTENTS

For Stefanie and Joanna

Wimbledon
Windmill

Wimbledon
Common

INTRODUCTION

Wimbledon, a busy London suburb inevitably evokes thoughts of the Tennis Championship but first and foremost it is a charming, centuries-old Surrey village. Its High Street is packed with traditional English pubs, elegant boutiques, shops, riding stables and handsome period villas and mansions, and even today has not lost its rural feel. A short trip down Wimbledon Hill leads to Wimbledon town with its main street, the Broadway. Several well known shops, restaurants, stylish wine bars and cafés offer a wide and diverse choice of food and goods, while theatres, cinemas and museums offer lively cultural life. Wimbledon Common, a vast area of woodland and heathland on the edge of the village is a great open space for walkers, golfers or horse riders. The Common is a Special Area of Conservation and Site of Special Scientific Interest thriving with wildlife. Other green areas in Wimbledon are Cannizaro Park, South Park Gardens, Holland Gardens and Wimbledon Park, all bordering the All England Lawn Tennis and Croquet Club. The Club is home to the Wimbledon Tennis Championship, a sport that rapidly changed from a social pastime to an international event, gathering huge crowds in Wimbledon every year. The name Wimbledon, or as it was formerly known, Wimmeldon, Wymmeldon, Wymelton, Wymbeldon, Wimbledone and Wimbleton means "Wynnman's Hill". The area of Wimbledon has been inhabited since prehistoric times; countless Palaeolithic and Neolithic scrapers, flakes, pots and implements have been found in many local barrows indicating that people settled here, cut down forests and cultivated crops.

Rushmere Pond on the Green

On the Common, the fortress misleadingly called "Caesar's Camp" dates from the Iron Age; however, there is no evidence that Romans actually occupied Wimbledon. The fort was previously called "The Rounds" and the new name stuck only in Victorian times. "The Rounds" enclosed area of 12 acres dates to 700 BC. It was most probably a fortified market with some huts for tribal leaders. Wimbledon was first mentioned in 967 in the charter signed by King Edgar the Peaceful. In the Domesday Book, Wimbledon was not mentioned, but was most likely a part of the Manor of Mortlake, which was owned by the Archbishops of Canterbury. In 1398, the unfortunate Archbishop Thomas Arundel fell out of favour with the king and the manor became Crown property. It was then granted by reigning monarchs to many people: Thomas Cromwell, Earl of Essex, Catherine Parr, Cardinal Reginald Pole, Christopher Hatton and most significantly to William Cecil, the Secretary of State to Queen Elizabeth I. The Cecil family changed the fate of Wimbledon. William's country retreat, the Old Rectory situated next to St Mary's church was visited by many courtiers; new roads were built and work was provided for many people. William stimulated the local economy significantly, but his son, Thomas, first Earl of Exeter transformed the village even more. In the year 1588 he built a new magnificent Elizabethan manor house surrounded by gardens and park, where he entertained sovereigns and nobility. Within a few years Wimbledon became an important social centre of Elizabethan and Stuart England and drew here some leading families. Providing jobs for locals, building roads and developing the village gave Thomas Cecil the name of "Maker of Wimbledon". By the seventeenth century, Wimbledon had grown considerably. Coaching services became available and the "Wimbledon machine", the first short-stage coach that took passengers to London was situated outside the Rose and Crown pub in the High Street. In 1613 Robert Bell of the East India Company built Eagle House at the top of High Street.

This beautiful Jacobean manor house with a Dutch-style gabled roof passed through many hands and today, immaculately restored is cared for by Al-Furqan Islamic Heritage Foundation. Wimbledon became fully established as a desirable location for grand and rich families and many large houses were built here in the seventeenth and eighteenth century: Chester House, West Side House, Wimbledon House, Cannizaro House, Spencer House, Marlborough House, the Kier, Wimbledon House and Wimbledon Park House. In the heart of the community is St Mary's church, the only Wimbledon church until 1859. It is a focal point that everybody recognises from the Wimbledon Tennis Championship coverage on the television. The beautiful late Gothic revival style church at the top of the hill, offering splendid views across Wimbledon, is Grade II listed. It was rebuilt three times, in the thirteenth century, eighteenth century and in the nineteenth century. There are some medieval remains of the chancel and some Georgian brickwork within the church. Inside there are numerous monuments and notable stained glass windows. In the churchyard there are many old mausoleums and tombs.

Top left: The Eagle House on High Street
Left: Wimbledon High Street by night
Opposite, top: Corner of Ridgway and High Street
Opposite, left: High Street
Opposite right: War Memorial, the Green

The biggest boost to the development of the area came during the nineteenth century when in 1838 the London and South Western Railway was introduced. Travel to suburban Wimbledon became fast and easy. The rural character of the area attracted more people to settle or open businesses here. Many farms, parks and large houses were sold as building land, and Victorian villas and terraced houses were built, followed by shops catering for this new community. By the 1880s, not only the village but also the new town of Wimbledon, had been established. The modern Elys Department Store, Police Station, and Library were opened in the 1870s and in the 1880s and 1890s NatWest Bank and the New Fire Station.

Above: Horse riders on Wimbledon Common
Left: Bluegate gravel pit on Wimbledon Common

Over the centuries, many famous people lived in Wimbledon: William and Thomas Cecil, Katherine Parr, Cardinal Pole, the Spencers, Lord Nelson, Lady Hamilton, William Wilberforce (the slave abolisher), Lord Rockingham (the celebrated Whig minister of George III), Lord Greville, Charles James Fox, Frederick Marryat (the novelist), Robert Bell (director of the East India Company), Sir Joseph Bazalgette (responsible for London's drainage system and for the Thames Embankment), Joseph Toynbee (surgeon, ear specialist), Duchess of Vendome (sister of the King of the Belgians), Thomas Hughes (author of *Tom Brown's School Days*), Sir Bartle Frere (governor of Bombay and Cape Colony), John Murray (the publisher); Sir Joseph Norman Lockyer (astronomer and discoverer of helium), Thomas Ralph Merton (phycisist), Charles Watson-Wentworth (Prime Minister), Eliza Cook (sentimental poet); Oliver Reed (the actor), James Hunt (Formula I Champion), Vinnie Jones (footballer and actor), Boris Becker (tennis player and Wimbledon Tournament winner) and many more.

Canizzaro Park

An important part of their lives as well as that of ordinary Wimbledonians is played out on Wimbledon Common. It is a green area comprising thick woodland with the rest made up of heath and grassland. Within the Common there are nine "meres" or lakes, some of them dating back to the Middle Ages. The soil of the Common was too poor for cultivating but provided pasture for the animals of the tenants and was a source of firewood as well as timber. As the Common was in rather a poor state in the nineteenth century, the Spencer family, ancestors of the late Diana, Princess of Wales, decided in 1864 to enclose a large area of the park and to sell a large portion of the Common for development. Following strong local opposition, the fifth Earl gave up his rights to the land. In compensation, Earl Spencer and his descendants had been receiving 1200 pounds a year until 1968 when a lump sum was paid. The Common was preserved in its natural condition under the Act of Parliament of 1871. It became a favourite recreational area used by walkers, golfers, bikers and horse riders. Another important part in the life of residents was a new tournament, little known to start with. Organised by the All England Croquet and Lawn Tennis Club, the Lawn Tennis Championship has changed the fate of Wimbledon dramatically. The All England Lawn Tennis and Croquet Club is a private club founded in 1868 in Nursery Road, off Worple Road. The first tennis championship attracted a few hundred spectators but within a very short time it became one of the biggest sporting events, not only in England, but in the whole world. The club moved to its current location in 1922, as the championship was rapidly outgrowing Nursery Road. The new grounds cover 42 acres and currently 19 courts are used during Wimbledon Fortnight. It attracts an attendance of nearly 500,000 people.

Opposite: The Stag House and St Mary's church
The Crooked Billet and Hand in Hand pubs

The nineteenth century trend of selling large estates and redeveloping them into smaller houses continued in the twentieth century. Wimbledon became a municipal borough in 1905 and in 1931 the Town Hall was built. After the war there was a major reorganisation of local government and the London Borough of Merton incorporated Wimbledon. The town expanded fast, especially alongside Worple Road and Ridgway through to Raynes Park. Wimbledon's biggest claim to fame may well be the annual tennis tournament, but there are other worthy attractions: New Wimbledon Theatre – an Edwardian theatre on Broadway; Polka Theatre – a children's theatre and arts centre; the new Centre Court Shopping Centre that incorporated the unused Town Hall; Wimbledon Common forest and heathland; a beautifully preserved Windmill from 1817; Cannizaro Park landscaped garden on the edge of Wimbledon Common which stages shows in the open air theatre; Merton Abbey Mills with its shops and the riverside pub; Deen City Farm with various farm animals and stables; Buddhapadipa Buddhist Temple in Collone Street; Wimbledon Greyhound and Stock Car Racing Stadium of 1928 offering dog racing and speedway; Wimbledon Lawn Tennis Museum housing all things tennis related; the Eagle House – a Jacobean house off the High Street, now home to the All Furquan Islamic Heritage Foundation; Southside House, a fascinating pre-Georgian house; The Village Club of 1859 housing a local museum; the eighteenth century King's College School with grand hall; and last but not least Wimbledon Park, the second largest park in the Merton area, previously the land of Wimbledon Manor. All these combine to make Wimbledon a dream place to live and visit.

The Broadway by night

FROM SOUTHSIDE HOUSE TO CAESAR'S CAMP

Southside House

Southside House stands on the southern corner of Wimbledon in Woodhayes Road, next to Kings College School. The house, an amalgamation of a Tudor farmhouse, Holme Lodge and Belvedere House was rebuilt by Robert Pennington in 1687. It is truly a gem and very popular with period film makers. A Dutch architect designed the house in the style of William and Mary. Hidden behind tall walls, one can only glimpse the statue of Plenty and Spring guarding the entrance to the house. Traditional in style, the house remains largely unchanged since its seventeenth-century origins. It is a treasure trove full of art, historical objects, seventeenth-century furniture and family memorabilia. Among many precious paintings are works of art by Van Dyck, Reynolds, Lawrence and other notable painters. The house is still used as a private residence by descendants of the Pennington family. The house has been visited by many famous people in the past – Queen Anne Boleyn, Marie Antoinette, Frederick, Prince of Wales, Lord Byron, Lord Nelson and Lady Emma Hamilton. Southside House underwent substantial restoration after World War II thanks to the efforts of Malcolm Munthe who devoted a lot of his time reinstating the house to its previous grandeur. Today, his children continue his good work of looking after the house through the Pennington-Mellor-Munthe Charity Trust. Southside House holds many attractions for visitors not only inside, but also outside. The immaculately cared for garden is full of surprises like secret pathways, classical follies and carefully created sculptured rooms demonstrating the talent and eccentricities of many generations of Pennington descendants. Concerts, workshops, lectures and various educational activities are also organised here.

This page and opposite: Southside House in Woodhayes Road

King's College School

King's College School

King's College School, a selective independent school is located on the southside of Wimbledon Common. To start with, the school occupied premises on the Strand in London, but moved to Wimbledon in 1897 when its headmaster bought some land here and a famous architect, Sir Banister Fletcher, designed the school buildings and the Great Hall. The hall, in neo-perpendicular style with the high gable, two red brick wings and ornamental parapets, is characteristic of Victorian architecture. The hall is one of the largest in England. During the war, the Great Hall was partially damaged during the Wimbledon bombing.

The Crooked Billet

Opposite Southside House, across a large stretch of green there is the charming Crooked Billet Road with a group of seventeenth-century cottages and two quintessentially English pubs. The Crooked Billet pub located at 14-16 Crooked Billet was built in 1776, but there has been an ale house on this site since 1509. The pub has a real sense of history inside, heavy old oaks beams, uneven parquet flooring, medieval flagstones, windows paned with cloudy glass. It is a cosy and welcoming place, popular with local residents and visitors alike, despite a resident ghost – an old Irish woman haunting the cellars! Roaring log fires in winter, picnics on the Green in summer and charming courtyards provide the perfect setting for a drink. The Hand in Hand pub residing at 6-11 Crooked Billet was originally a bakery and was taken over by one of the ancestors of the Watneys brewing dynasty. Since 1835, the pub has offered a good selection of drinks and food. A small courtyard at the entrance and low ceilings give this pub a distinctive atmosphere of a local country pub. The grass area outside is shared by both pubs and in the summer people gather here in their hundreds for a drink. Not to be outdone by the Crooked Billet, the Hand in Hand pub also has a ghost! With such an awesome location and traditional character of the pubs, it is not difficult to understand the popularity of these places. Nearby the Gothic Lodge at Woodhayes Road was built in 1763. The house depicts distinctive features of the eighteenth century "Gothic style" popularised by Horace Walpole at Strawberry Hill. The longest inhabitant of the Gothic Lodge was Sir William Preece, the Chief Post Office Engineer. He was famous for his many experiments with electricity; his home was the first in London that was wired for electric power and telecommunications. William Preece was also responsible for the installation of street lighting in the Wimbledon area.

Above right: The Crooked Billet pub
Middle right: Hand in Hand pub
Bottom right: Gothic Lodge at Woodhayes Road

Westside Common

There are many imposing houses alongside Westside Common, but Chester House is one of the oldest and most historic houses in Wimbledon. This Grade II listed building situated on top of Wimbledon Hill at Westside Common, was most probably built circa 1680. Chester House was substantially extended and altered in the nineteenth century, but the original outline of the house is still clearly visible. The most well known owner of the house was John Horne-Tooke, who resided here from 1792 until 1812. A politician and champion of radical political reforms, after the French Revolution started, he was suspected of trying to start a revolution in England. He was arrested, but after a short court case, acquitted. Highly controversial were not only his political views but also his plans to add a mausoleum at the back of the house. Fortunately for the future inhabitants, his plans were changed by his heirs. He is buried in the churchyard of St Mary's church in Ealing. At the beginning of the twentieth century due to the bad state of repair, Chester House was threatened with demolition. Luckily Barclays Bank bought the place just before the Second World War and converted it into its head office. Today, the house has been lovingly restored to its former glory. Another interesting house, the Kier at 24 West side Common is an imposing house built in 1789 by the Portuguese family, the Aquilars. The main wing of the house is three storeys and it has a Greek Doric porch. The second owners, the family of the Brays set up a Roman Catholic Chapel here. The name of the house, the Kier meaning fort, was given much later in the second part of the nineteenth century, when the house was transformed into a school. Just across the road, the cottages in the middle of West Place were built and rented in 1849 by Daniel Mason. Round the corner, the Fox and Grape pub at 9 Camp Road is stuck in an enclave of houses on the edge of Wimbledon Common. It was opened in 1837 as a union beer shop. The first landlord was William Fisher. From 1868 for the next 20 years it was used as changing rooms by Wimbledon Football Club. The place retained much of its original charm coupled with a modern edge.

The Kier

Westside Common

Chester House

Cannizaro Park

Cannizaro Park is a beautiful landscaped garden on the edge of Wimbledon Common adjacent to the now Cannizaro Hotel. The park is bounded by Westside Common, Royal Wimbledon Golf Course, Dunstall Road and Camp Road. This well loved and popular park is famous for its many mature maples, redwoods, beeches, pines and the collection of rhododendrons. Cannizaro ornamental gardens cover some 35 acres of land. It used to be a private garden established around Warren House built in the early 1700s in Queen Anne Style. Former residents include home secretary Henry Dundas, 1st Viscount Melville; Thomas Walker close friend of Britain's first Prime Minister Sir Robert Walpole; and John Lyde-Brown the governor of the Bank of England. Henry Dundas made the place famous by throwing lavish parties during which he often discussed political problems with Prime Minister William Pitt. Another frequent guest here was King George III. Lady Jane Wood was created by Henry Dundas in memory of his wife, Lady Jane Hope. The name Cannizaro dates back to the early nineteenth century. Francis Platamone, Count St Antonio, a British subject of Sicilian birth and his wife Sophia, sister of George Johnstone, leased Warren House. Sophia was a great collector of music and patron of musicians. In their house, they entertained Maria Fitzherbert, the wife of George IV, Countess Esterhazy, the wife of the Austrian Ambassador, the Duke of Wellington and many other important people. Francis succeeded to the dukedom of Cannizaro in Sicily in 1832 and swiftly returned to Italy while his wife remained in the house until her death in 1841. Distinguished visitors in the nineteenth century included royalty and famous writers – Lord Tennyson, Oscar Wilde and Henry James. Possibly the best features of the garden were created by the Wilson family between 1920 and 1940. After that, the house was sold to the Borough Council in 1947 and the gardens were opened to the public and in the later part of the twentieth century, greatly improved. New features include the Water Garden, Belvedere, the Sunken Garden and last but not least the Italian Garden. In 1987, the house was sold by Merton Borough Council and turned into a hotel. The park is listed in the English Heritage Register of Parks and Gardens of Special Historic Interest as Grade II and has an outstanding collection of trees and shrubs. In the summer, there are open air concerts here as well as exhibitions. The park is graced by two statues: one, a classical sculpture of Diana and the Fawn, and the other is a bust of Emperor Haile Selassie of Ethiopia. Slightly hidden behind the trees, in the area of the old tennis court, the latter is a popular place of pilgrimage for the Rastafarian community, who worship Haile Selassie as God's incarnation. He stayed in Wimbledon when he was exiled from his country in 1935 during Italy's invasion of Ethiopia. In 1996 a group of local residents set up the voluntary organisation, "Friends of Cannizaro Park" to help with the running and maintenance of the park.

Opposite, top: Millenium Fountain in Cannizaro Park
Opposite, left: Garden details in Cannizaro Park; right: Cannizaro Hotel Terrace in Cannizaro Park

Aviary in Cannizaro Park

Sunken Garden in Cannizaro Park

Clockwise from top left: Maple tree leaf in Cannizaro Park; Cannizaro Hotel;
Maple tree leaf on the bench in Cannizaro Park; Haile Selassie statue in Cannizaro Park
Opposite: Cannizaro Park

Top left: Diana and the Fawn
statue in Cannizaro Park

Left: Garden details in
Cannizaro Park

Opposite: The pond in
Cannizaro Park

Above: Autumn in Cannizaro Park
Left: The Gothic House in Cannizaro Park

Right: Winter blizzard in Cannizaro Park
Below: First snow in Cannizaro Park

The Round School

The Round School, also known as William Wilberforce School, at 19 Camp Road was built in 1758 as a charity school. The school house which is of a characteristic octagonal shape and steeply pitched tiled roof was built thanks to the generosity of local gentry. William Wilberforce was one of the first governors, and Joseph Andrews and Sarah Andrews the first schoolmaster and schoolmistress. Fifty to seventy poor children up to the age of twelve could learn how to write and read here. In 1813, the school became the National School, later on, the Central School, the William Wilberforce School and finally the Study Preparatory school.

Above: The Round School
Right and opposite: Wimbledon Common Golf Club

Wimbledon Common Golf Club

The Wimbledon Common Golf Club was established in 1908 as "The Wimbledon Town Golf Club". The club's founders were H D Dormer, HV Ely, GJ Booth and Henry Chaplin. Soon after permission to play on the Common was given from the Conservators, the natural woodland course was designed by Tom Dunn. The course is built on flat heath land and parkland and has no sand bunkers. Over the years the club prospered and increased the number of members from 100 at the time of establishment to 250 in 1990. In the year 1919, two clubs, "Wimbledon Town Golf Club" and "The South London Golf Club" amalgamated and the new name of "Wimbledon Common Golf Club" was decided upon. During both world wars, golf couldn't be played as the Common was taken over by the military. After the war, the club gradually recovered despite facing many challenges and with the necessary improvements and careful maintenance it became a hugely successful club with 300 members.

Caesar's Camp

Caesar's Camp on the hilltop of the south-west side of the Common is an Iron Age circular fort. Dated to about 700 BC, the settlement enclosed some twelve acres of land and it was most possibly a trade centre and the tribal home. It was surrounded by a nine metres wide and four metres deep ditch and two walls. Inside the camp there are traces of round huts. Despite the name, there is no evidence that the Romans ever occupied Wimbledon. In earlier centuries, the fort was called "Bensbury" and "The Rounds". Today the fort is a Scheduled Ancient Monument, but it is not easy to find as the ramparts were significantly reduced in height by John Samuel Sawbridge-Erle-Drax in 1870. He planned to use this area for building houses; luckily further destruction to the ancient settlement was stopped by strong local opposition led by Sir Henry Peek. As he played an important role in the local community, his name has been inscribed on the stones surrounding nearby Caesar's Well. The well located some four hundred yards north of the fort has been used from prehistoric times. The original well dried up suddenly in 1911, but the spring a few feet down the hill continues to flow. Caesar's Fort is within the boundary of Royal Wimbledon Golf Club.

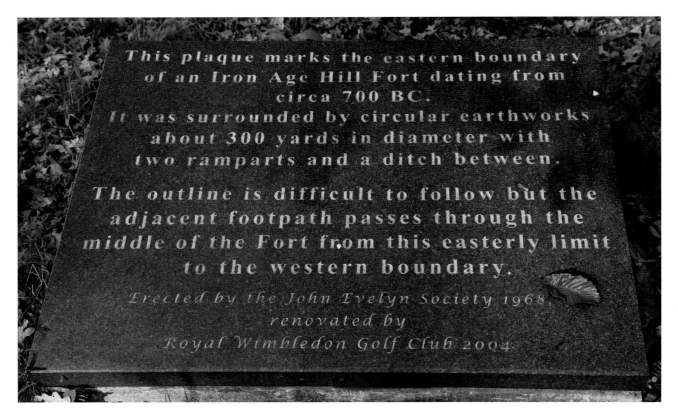

Royal Wimbledon Club

The Royal Wimbledon Club is situated on the south-west side of Wimbledon Common. The game of golf was introduced to England in the year 1603 by King James I from Scotland. Played informally by courtiers, it was only in the nineteenth century that it started to be played in Wimbledon. Members of the London Scottish Rifle Volunteers established the London Scottish Golf Club in Wimbledon in 1864. Originally limited to seven holes, the course designed by Tom Dunn was expanded to an eighteen hole course in 1871. In 1881, a group of civilian members broke away from the club and formed Wimbledon Club. The name was changed to Royal Wimbledon Club in 1882. Until 1907 both clubs shared the same course, but in 1907 land was leased from Warren Farm and a new course was designed by Willie Park Jnr. The course was later redesigned in 1924 by Harry Colt.

Right: Royal Wimbledon Golf Club
Opposite: Caesar's Camp plaque

Top: Caesar's Well
Above: Springwell cottage on Wimbledon Common
Left: Forest near Caesar's Well

FROM WIMBLEDON WINDMILL TO WIMBLEDON PARK

Wimbledon Common

Wimbledon Common is one of London's biggest green open spaces, criss-crossed by footpaths and horse tracks. The Common which comprises parts of Wimbledon, Putney and Kingston-upon-Thames comprises about 460 hectares of woodland, scrubland, heathland, bogs and grassland. The Common is home to a large variety of birds, animals and plant life. The land is protected by the Wimbledon and Putney Commons Act of 1871 and most of the area is a site of Special Interest and a Special Area of Conservation. There are many different land uses of the Common: golf, horse-riding, walking, and football. The Common is governed by a body of Conservators; five elected by local residents and 3 by Government Departments, run by over 20 staff. It played an important role in the history of Wimbledon Village. The land, despite the misleading name was not public property but belonged to the Lord of the Manor. Tenants of the lord were allowed to collect firewood and timber for building houses, as well as graze a limited number of their animals. Stray animals or those grazed without authorisation were impounded in the special fenced off area called the pound. One of them can still be found between the Green and the Parkside. The Common

was not nice or safe in previous centuries; rubbish was often dumped here and it was a favourite hunting ground for highwaymen, gypsies, escaped convicts and vagrants. Throughout the seventeenth and eighteenth century it was also a favourite duelling ground for affronted noblemen. Even though duelling was illegal, it continued into the nineteenth century. The very famous last duel was between James Brudnell, Earl of Cardigan and Captain Harvey Tuckett; it caused uproar in society and discredited duelling as the earl used a hair trigger which was not honourable. In 1864, Earl Spencer announced his intention to enclose 700 acres of this area and build himself a new manor house on the site occupied by the windmill with the intention of selling the rest for development purposes. This plan however created strong local opposition and after four years of legal disputes, the new Wimbledon and Putney Commons Act secured the Common as open, unenclosed and unbuilt natural land. In 1916 an airfield was set up on Wimbledon Common and fighter aircraft of 141 Squadron of 49 wing, used the grassy plain between Parkside and the Windmill as the runway. Today the Common is a wildlife oasis as well as a favourite recreational area.

Wimbledon Windmill

The symbol and the most prominent feature of the Common is the Windmill, which is preserved as a museum. It was built in 1817 by Charles March, a Roehampton carpenter, as a hollow post mill. In 1864, it was converted into living accommodation for Common keepers; it was rebuilt again in 1893 as a smock mill, since which time it has been a museum. The mill underwent further restorations in 1957 and 1975. It has double patent sails and is winded by a fantail, and the mill machinery is still intact. Lord Baden Powell, founder of the Boy Scout movement spent time here in 1908 writing his book *Scouting for Boys*. The windmill museum details the history of this windmill and depicts the development of windmills in Britain. English and French millstones as well as some farm machinery are displayed outside the windmill. During the summer months, it is open on Saturdays and Sundays. Next to the windmill is a tea room and the car park.

Wimbledon Windmill

The London Scottish Golf Club

The headquarters of the London Scottish Golf Club is the cottage at the back of the Windmill. Until 1871, membership was restricted mainly to Scottish and volunteers' corps. Since new civilian members joined the club, there were a lot of disagreements and finally in 1881 civilian members parted company and established the Royal Wimbledon Club. As the course is in the public area, golfers need to give people right of way as well as wear red coats, a rule introduced in 1892.

Wimbledon Windmill and London Scottish Golf Club course

Wimbledon
Windmill
and the cottage

Agricultural
machinery
outside the
cottage

Horse trough

Windmill parts

Wimbledon Common Ponds

There are nine ponds in the Wimbledon Common area. The best known is Rushmere, which is situated on the Village Green. The Bluegate Gravel Pit can be found along Parkside. The narrow channel dividing this elongated gravel pit gives the impression of two individual ponds, especially during hot summers when part of the pit dries up. The pond is surrounded by mature silver birch and oak trees and on its edge grow willows and soft rushes. Hookhamslade Pond is situated on the eastern side of the Common, off Parkside. Seven Post Pond can also be found along Parkside, and it is yet another gravel pit. In the past it was used by waggoners. The wooden wheels would expand in the water enabling a perfect fit for the iron rims. Ravine Pond is quite new, as it was created to celebrate the Millennium. Queensmere, a short walk down from the Windmill is deeper than any of the other ponds, being impounded in a small valley. It was made circa 1887 and covers approximately 2 acres. All of the ponds support diverse aquatic flora and fauna: yellow irises, white water lilies, gipsy wort, greater spearwort, and marsh penny wort all of which grow commonly and support a surprisingly rich variety of insects, including dragonflies and damselflies which thrive in such conditions.

Queensmere Pond

Clockwise from top left: Swan on Queensmere Pond; frozen Queensmere Pond; Bluegate Gravel Pit; frozen Queensmere Pond
Opposite: Bluegate Gravel Pit

Bluegate Gravel Pit

Opposite: Mixed trees on
Wimbledon Common

Birches on
Wimbledon Common

Wimbledon Common Woods

"He does not know Wimbledon Common who is not familiar with its labyrinths of leafy glades, its tangled thickets of wild red rose, bramble and honeysuckle; who has not often traversed its turfy plateau and had the perfume of odoriferous herbs borne in upon his senses." Walter Johnson: *Wimbledon Common, its Geology, Antiquities and Natural History*, 1912. The woodland forms a substantial part of the Common. Of approximately one million trees on the Common, the most populous are: Oak, Birch, Platanus x, Horse Chestnut, Common Lime, Sycamore, Acer, Norwegian Maple, Hazel, Beech and Aspen. Woodland is an important habitat for animals and 22 species of mammals, 3 species of amphibians, 3 species of reptiles and many birds were observed on the Common. Common mammals are: hedgehogs, moles, shrews, rabbits, voles, foxes, mice, stoats, weasels, badgers, ferrets and Muntjac. Almost a hundred different species of birds have been recorded here: mute swans, common geese, mallards, fire crests, egrets, Kingfishers, and Winchats. The woods are also inhabited by six species of bats. Wimbledon Common also supports 24 butterfly species and many other insects.

Top left: Horse riders on the Plain

Centre left: Mixed woods of Wimbledon Common

Bottom left: Bluegate Ride on Wimbledon Common

Opposite: Morning mist on the Common

Top left: Morning mist on the Common

Opposite: Common's path

Bottom left: Forest stream

All England Lawn Tennis and Croquet Club

The All England Lawn Tennis and Croquet Club is a private club founded in 1868 by John Walsh, the editor of the *Field*, and some enthusiasts of croquet R F Dalton, J Hinde Hale, A Law, S H Clarke Maddock and Walter Jones Whitmore. They elected themselves as the first committee and the original name of the club was the All England Croquet Club. The club was located off Worple Road. Lawn tennis, originally called "Sphairistike" was introduced in 1875 by Major Walter Clapton Wingfield. The game was derived from court tennis, called real tennis but unlike its predecessor, it could be played anywhere, and there was no need for expensive inside courts. His outdoor game proved to be not only less complicated than real tennis, but also more interesting and energetic. He was a very good entrepreneur and thanks to his well thought promotions, it was an immediate success. In 1870 a club pavilion was built and in 1875 one croquet ground was set apart for tennis and badminton. During 1876 the All England Club devoted itself increasingly to the new game. In 1877 during a general meeting of the club it was agreed that the club name would be changed to All England Croquet and Lawn Tennis Club. The first Tennis Championship took place in the same year to raise money to repair the broken pony roller, which was essential for the upkeep of the lawn; competitors paid one guinea to enter and spectators, all 200 of them, one shilling. The very same roller can still be seen in the corner of Centre Court today. The rackets at this time were snow–shoe shaped and heavier than today. The net was five feet high but dipped in the middle to three feet three inches. Scoring points was a bit of a novelty, as the 15 points up system of the Marylebone Cricket Club governing cricket and lawn tennis was rejected and 15, 30, 40, deuce and advantage were introduced. In the year 1883, 2,500 spectators watched the challenge round. The popularity of the sport grew rapidly not only because of the game but also because of the strong personalities of the early players. A few years later, the Championship drew a one thousand strong crowd. In the year 1884 Ladies Singles and Gentlemen's Doubles were added and in 1913, Ladies Doubles. The famous colours of the club, purple and dark green were introduced in 1909. In 1913/1914 there were 3,500 spaces for spectators. The increasing pressure of crowds and traffic problems proved that there was a need for relocation. The move to bigger quarters was postponed by World War I, but in 1922, the club moved to its present position at Church Road. The new club was bold in its modernity. The ground covered 13.5 acres and boasted 19 tennis courts. It was opened by King George V and Queen Mary. Today, the club has 375 full members and 100 temporary playing members as well as some honorary members. The patron of the club is Her Majesty the Queen, while H.R.H. the Duke of Kent is the President. The Wimbledon Championship runs under the joint management of the All England Lawn Tennis Croquet Club and the Lawn Tennis Association. It is the only Grand Slam tennis event still held on grass. Today the club ground covers 42 acres and it consists of the Millennium Building with facilities for players, press, officials and members, a museum, a shop, 19 tournament courts, 16 other grass courts, 5 red shale courts, 3 continental clay courts, 1 American clay court and 5 indoor courts. The most important court, Centre Court was built in 1922 but has been extended several times and today seats 15,000 people. It is re-sown every year and used only for the championships. Since 2009 it has a retractable roof, which is made of translucent material allowing natural light to reach the grass. Court Number 1 was built in 1997 and seats just over 11,000 spectators. Despite the prediction of the first winner, that "lawn tennis will never rank among our great games", it has become one of the most popular sports and the Championship, the most prestigious event in the world attracting some 450,000 people over two weeks in late June and early July as well as viewers in more than 150 countries. The Championship is played on grass courts and all players are required to wear white. The five main events of the Championship include Gentlemen's Singles, Ladie's Singles, Gentlemen's Doubles, Ladie's Doubles and Mixed Doubles. Junior events include Boys' Singles, Girls' Singles, Boys' Doubles and Girls' Doubles. The tickets for the event are allocated through a lottery system, but there are also some hospitality packages that can be bought. The famous long queues outside the club are for court tickets that go on sale on the day. There are also so-called ground tickets which allow you to wonder around the grounds, take in the atmosphere, watch the matches on big TV screens; all that while sipping champagne and eating strawberries and cream. This quintessential English tradition started in the 1870s; strawberries signalled the arrival of summer and it coincided with the tournament. The first person however to pair berry with dairy was Cardinal Wolsey in the 1500s. So popular is this Wimbledon snack that during the Championship, more than 27,000 kilos of strawberries and 7,000 litres of cream are eaten!

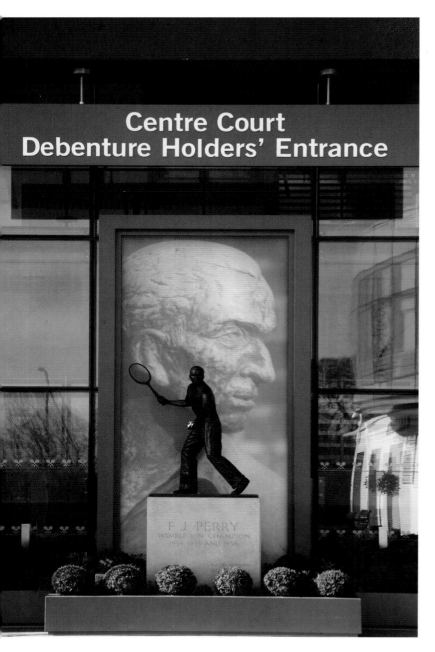

Centre Court
Debenture Holders' Entrance

F J PERRY
WIMBLEDON CHAMPION
1934 1935 AND 1936

A.E.L.T.C

Left: Fred Perry statue by the Centre Court
Top: AELTC decorative gate donated by Reverent WV Doherty
Above: AELTC decorative wall
Opposite, top: Forming the queue for ground tickets
Opposite, bottom left: Strawberries and cream
Opposite, bottom right: Tennis fans waiting for tickets

All England Lawn Tennis and Croquet Club

Wimbledon Tennis Museum

Wimbledon Lawn Tennis Museum

The Wimbledon Lawn Tennis Museum is located at the All England Lawn Tennis Association Headquarters at Church Road. Originally opened in 1977, it was relocated, significantly modernised and reopened by HRH the Duke of Kent in 2006. The museum shows the history of tennis from its origins to the present day through the museum's latest interactive consoles, 200 degree cinema screen showing films demonstrating the effect of tennis on the human body and guided tours accompanied by a three-dimensional ghost-like image of John McEnroe reminiscing about his tennis career. There are also more traditional displays and an amazing collection of tennis memorabilia from the very early times to the most recent. The collections include tennis outfits, championship trophies, personal belongings and a vast selection of rackets. The museum's Kenneth Ritchie Library boasts a huge collection of books, periodicals and videos relating to lawn tennis; all these materials are available to visitors by appointment only. Guided tours take visitors behind the scenes of the club to Centre Court, Court Number 1, the Water Gardens, the Millennium Building, the Press Interview Room and BBC's Television Station.

Wimbledon Park

Situated in a lovely valley created by the last Ice Age, Wimbledon Park with its placid boating lake is a beautiful urban park. It is overlooked by the spire of St Mary's church and covers about 400 acres comprising the grounds of the seat of the Manor of Wimbledon and has been owned by a succession of wealthy landowners. The Elizabethan manor house completed here in 1588 by Sir Thomas Cecil was admired and envied by many. In 1638 Charles I bought the manor for Queen Henrietta Maria and the house was later sold to George Digby, the Earl of Bristol and in 1712 to Theodore Jannsen, a director of the South Sea Company. Jannsen had to sell it in 1728 to Sarah, Duchess of Marlborough, after the spectacular crash of his company. Sarah demolished Janssen's unfinished house and built a new one. Her grandson John Spencer improved the place, followed by his son, Earl Spencer who commissioned in 1765 Capability Brown, the most famous of all English landscape architects, to turn Wimbledon Park Valley from Renaissance garden into a classic English garden. The large lake in the middle of the park was formed by constructing the dam across the brook. The land was transformed into one of the most beautiful parks in England. Unfortunately nothing remains of Wimbledon Park Manor, as it burned down in 1785. The only remnant of the grandeur of the estate is the Artesian Well that was built by Earl Spencer to supply water to Wimbledon Park House. The Artesian Well at 19 Arthur Road was converted into a dwelling in 1975. It is easily recognisable by its octagonal shape with a domed cement roof. Since 1815 due to a silting-up problem, the well stopped being used. Today it is a Grade II listed building. In 1846 the 4th Earl Spencer sold the estate to the property developer John Augustus Beaumont. The park was gradually decreased in size as the land was sold for redevelopment. In 1914 the Borough of Wimbledon bought the park and since then the park has been open to the public.

Playing fields in
Wimbledon Park

Wimbledon Park Lake

Wimbledon Park Lake

Café at Wimbledon Park

Above: Artesian Well House of Wimbledon Park House
Right: Wimbledon Park Lake

FROM ST MARY'S TO WIMBLEDON HIGH STREET

St Mary's Church

St Mary's church at 30 St Mary's Road is a Grade II listed building. There has been a church on the site since 950 AD. The building was a small wooden structure, most probably built by the Lord of the Manor, the Archbishop of Canterbury. The wooden church was rebuilt in stone in the late thirteenth century during the reign of Edward I. A medieval thirteenth century "Leper window", a small, low barred window used to administer the sacrament to the unwell who gathered outside can be found on the south side of the chancel. A fourteenth-century stained glass window showing St George has been moved to the Cecil Chapel from its original position on the north side of the chancel. Two out of the eight St Mary's bells are medieval. First, "St Bartholomew" was made in 1520 by London bell founder, William Culverden. The second one which has an inscription "Praise ye the Lord" was made in 1572. For centuries St Mary's was the only church in the village and it needed to be enlarged; it was rebuilt twice. The Cecil family residence in the Old Rectory and Elizabethan manor became strongly connected with Wimbledon village and with the church during the Reformation and Elizabethan era. The Gothic Cecil Chapel was built on the south side of the chancel by Sir Edward Cecil in the 1620s as his family mortuary chapel. Six windows commemorate his two wives and four daughters and each of the windows has his coat of arms with six lions. The simple black marble tomb stands in the centre of the chapel above the grave of Edward Cecil. With an increase in the population of Wimbledon, the church was rebuilt in 1788 in Georgian style according to the design of John Johnson. A new gallery, the north aisle and some pews were erected. Finally, in 1843 the church was rebuilt by Messrs. Scott and Moffat, a highly respected Victorian firm. Scott also designed St Pancras railway station and the Albert Memorial in Hyde Park.

St Mary's church was significantly enlarged with impressive Gothic windows and was encased in knapped flints which made the old and the new part look uniform. The square tower and copper spire of 196 feet high made the church visually dominant in the area. The clock on the tower was donated in 1877 by John Murray and the church organ was donated in 1843 by James Peache. In 1920 the Warrior Chapel was built. It is a memorial to all local residents who fought and died in the First and Second World Wars. Bronze tablets in the oak panelled walls contain the names of the fallen soldiers. Some of the oldest memorial tablets in the church include that of Philip Lewston who died in 1462, Katherine and William Walter, Sir Richard Wynn who died in 1649 and was a friend of Charles I, and Peter Shaw, MD physician to King George II and George III. Two modern brasses commemorate William Wilberforce, the slave trade abolitionist and Walter Reynolds, Lord Chancellor under Edward II and Archbishop of Canterbury in 1313. The most recent tablets are to Kathleen and Leslie Godfree, who were winners of the Wimbledon tennis tournament. All Wimbledonians were buried in the graveyard of St Mary's from the tenth century until 1882, when the Gap Road Cemetery was opened. Unfortunately most of the early graves have vanished and the earliest now date to the seventeenth century. Within the graveyard there are a number of large monuments, now Grade II listed buildings of special architectural interest. Some of them are: mausoleum of Sir Joseph William Bazalgette, William and Hannah Wilberforce,

John Hopkins, Joseph Marryat, Sir Theodore Janssen, Countess of Lucan and perhaps the most unusual, the pyramid tomb of Gerard de Visme, a son of the Huguenot family, the owner of Wimbledon Lodge, who died in 1797. The tomb is described by Pevsner in *Buildings of England* as: "pyramid of blocks of vermiculated rustication with corner acroteria to the base". The unusual shape of the tomb was most probably influenced by Napoleons' conquest of Egypt. In front of the church, as if guarding it, there is a Stag Lodge. It is a rather awkwardly positioned building, which was built in 1850 by Augustus Beaumont as a gate lodge to Wimbledon Park House. In 1872 the Manor House was sold and development of this area started. New streets, Arthur Road, Leopold Road, Home Park and Lake Road were laid out. Stag Lodge lost its function as a lodge but remained in its position. The original stag sculpture was placed on the building in 1881; it was replaced with an exact copy after being unfortunately damaged when removed for safe keeping during the Second World War.

Top left: St Mary's churchyard

Bottom left: Gerard de Visme tomb

Opposite, top left: Cross in St Mary's churchyard

Opposite, bottom left: Mausoleum of Sir Joseph William Bazalgette

Opposite, far right: Stag Lodge and St Mary's church

St Mary's church

St Mary's church clock

Right: St Mary's church

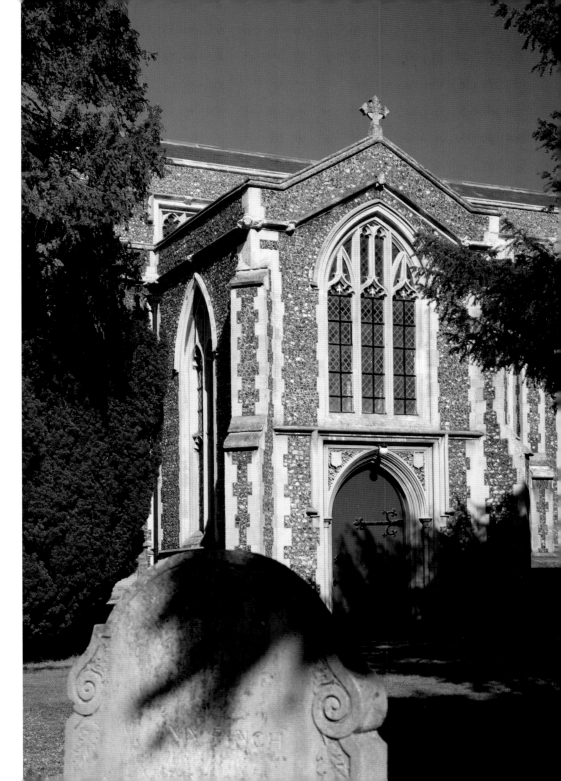

Old Rectory

Old Rectory at No 54 Church Road is Wimbledon's oldest building. The house was built in close proximity of St Mary's church in about 1500. It was the very first brick building in the area and it was more like a manor house than a parsonage house. The house consisted of lavish dining rooms, study rooms, ten bedrooms and wine cellars. There were also many outbuildings such as a dairy house, a bake house, a wash house, a granary, barns and stables for fourteen horses. Next to the house there were extensive gardens. As the house is set back from Church Road, it is not visible from the front but its impressive Tudor towers, chimney pots and crenellated roof can be glimpsed from within St Mary's churchyard. Originally owned by rich rectors of St Mary's church, later on it became the property of Henry VIII and was leased to courtiers. In 1546 the house was visited by Henry VIII; it was an unexpected visit, as during his tour of the Surrey properties, the king became seriously ill and needed some rest before returning to Whitehall. The Manor Grange of his last wife, Catherine Parr wasn't grand enough, so the Rectory was chosen. The most significant resident in the history of the house was William Cecil, Lord Burghley. He was Secretary of State in Edward VI's Council, later on, a chief adviser to Queen Elizabeth I, being Master of the Court of Wards and Liveries, Lord Treasurer and Chief Minister. His extensive Wimbledon house was run by a staff of twenty people. He took great care of the house as well as of the garden; most probably he was the one who established the famous Fig Walk there, one of only two known in England. The son of William Cecil, Thomas, returned here in the 1570s and started to build a grand Elizabethan manor house on a steep hill, to the east of the Old Rectory, on the site of the Old Mortlake Manor House. The new manor house completed in 1588 was stunning, with multilevel terraces and courtyards, a great hall and a chapel. The Old Rectory partly demolished and used only by the servants, lost its grandeur; however, unlike the Elizabethan manor, it survived. Restored and extended in the

nineteenth century it was returned to its former glory. Its connection with the past is not only through its fascinating architecture but also through a ghost – Henry VIII's ghost! He stayed here two weeks before his death and he must have liked it a lot, as his heavy footsteps are sometimes heard at night. Both William and Thomas Cecil played a great role in putting Wimbledon on the map. They hosted parties for Queen Elizabeth I and James I as well as powerful courtiers and Wimbledon slowly started to develop into a comfortable location not too far from London and the Royal Palace of Nonsuch.

Buddhapadipa Temple

Buddhapadipa Temple is situated at 14 Collone Road. It is the first Buddhist temple in the United Kingdom and one of only two in Europe. This stunning Wat Temple surrounded by lush gardens was built in a traditional Thai style in 1976 by the London Buddhist Temple Foundation. It became a formal Temple in 1982 after the celebration of a monastic boundary. The main aim of the Temple is to spread theoretical and practical Buddhist teaching. The building is highly ornamental. Red and gold decoration of the windows and roof are in striking contrast to the white walls. Inside, colourful surreal murals by Chalermchai Kasitppiat and Panya Vijinthanasarn depict the life of Buddha. Most impressive are the statues of Buddha in the great shrine. Visitors are also welcome to explore the gardens with the shady pond criss-crossed with scenic bridges. Scattered around the garden are messages of wisdom. The Temple and the garden give the impression of a far away Asian place rather than a leafy London suburb.

Above left: Temple architectural details; above centre and right: Statue at the entrance of Buddhapadipa Temple.
Opposite: Detail of Buddhapadipa Temple

Garden of
Buddhapadipa Temple

Buddhapadipa Temple

The Green

The Green lies very close to Wimbledon Village and the High Street. This vast green space was used by villagers for cattle grazing. On the edge of the Green is Rushmere Pond, the oldest pond on the Common. More than likely, the pond originated in medieval times and was the source of rushes for the villagers' thatching. The pond was an important source of water for cattle and horses. Horses were kept by the Lord of the Manor; his tenants followed his example and it is certain that horses were grazed on the Common. With the growing number of country retreats and residents in the village, the number of coaches and horse riders travelling across the Green and alongside Parkside to London increased significantly. In the late seventeenth century the trip from Wimbledon to London was dangerous, as the chance of encountering highwaymen was high. Jerry Abershawe was Wimbledon's highwayman. Jerry started as a driver of a post-chaise and at the age of 17 became a daring thief and a ringleader of highwaymen. People feared but also admired him, as there were plenty of anecdotes about his gallantry. As some sources say, he would not rob women or unarmed men. His colourful but short career finished in 1795 at the age of 22, when he was cornered by Bow Street Runners and sentenced to death. At his execution he put on a show of bravado; he kept up incessant conversations with the crowd, frequently laughed and at the final stage, he kicked off his boots to disprove his mother who often said that he would die in his shoes. Named by some historians as "the last highwayman", his story doesn't end here. His ghost, "A laughing Highwayman" rides from time to time on his phantom steed through Wimbledon Common and his horse's hooves can be heard from afar.

Horse riding became a past time and sport and many gentlemen took to the Common for daily exercise. A growing need for riding lessons brought William Cooke to this area. From 1866, he and later his son William, kept horses at the stables in Church Road. Other stables in Wimbledon were managed by William Kirkpatrick, originally at Marryat Road and from 1919 his new Hilcote Riding School was opened behind the Dog and Fox Pub. In 1980 the stables were reopened by new owners as Wimbledon Village Stables. With such an amount of horses in the area, there was also a need for a blacksmith; one of them was John Linton. He established himself in 1617 on the edge of the Green, at the corner of the High Street and Southside. The blacksmith remained in the same place well into the twentieth century.

The pound on the Green

Opposite: Rushmere Pond on the Green

Woods alongside Parkside Road

Drinking fountain at Parkside

Rushmere Pond on the Green

Opposite: Rushmere Pond on the Green

Above: War Memorial on the Green
Left: The Green

This page and opposite:
The annual Wimbledon Village
Fair on the Green

Eagle House

Eagle House situated on the High Street near the junction of Marryat Road is one of the finest examples of a Jacobean manor house. It was built in 1617 as a country retreat for Robert Bell, a wealthy City merchant and a co-founder of the British East India Company which at the time of establishment was colourfully called "The Society of Adventurers for the discovery of the trade for the East Indies". The activities of the company were not only restricted to trade but also covered government, administrative, ambassadorial and military functions. The house, set back from the High Street has got a highly characteristic double-gabled roof and imposing stone eagle statue. It was built of brick with stone quoins. Gardens at the back of the house were designed with great care; there were elegant flower beds and paths. After Bell's death, the house passed through many hands, until eventually it was purchased in 1789 by the Reverend Thomas Lancaster who transformed it into "Wimbledon School for Young Noblemen and Gentlemen". An important visit by Lord Nelson and Lady Hamilton influenced the owners to change the name of the school into "Nelson's Academy". Another famous name associated with the house is Arthur Schopenhauer, the philosopher who studied here in 1803. Careful restoration of the house in 1882 by the next owner, a well known architect, Thomas Graham Jackson saved many original features of the house, perhaps the most important being the seventeenth-century Delft tile work. Today the house is used as an office of Al-Furgan Islamic Heritage Foundation, a company preserving and documenting Islamic written heritage.

Above and opposite: Eagle House on High Street

Rose and Crown Pub on the High Street

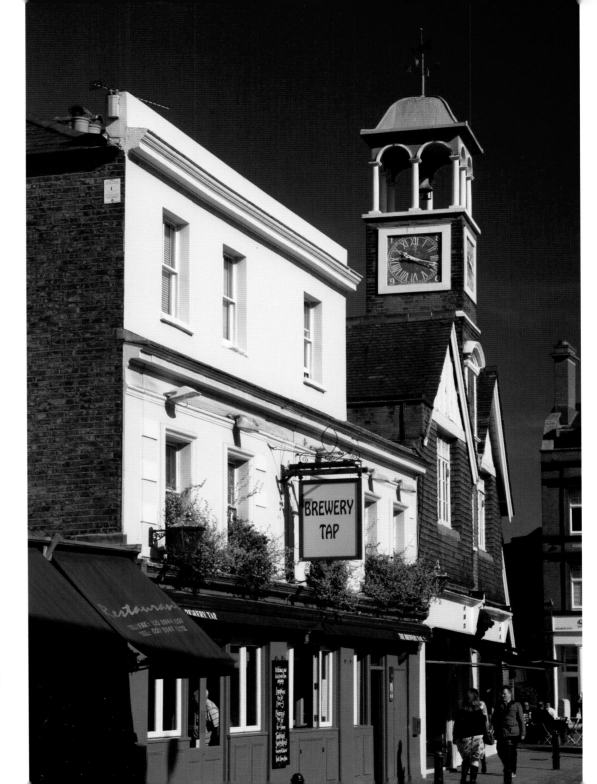

Brewery Tap restaurant on the High Street

Top: Maison St Cassien Café, High Street
Above: Barclays Bank, High Street
Left: Old Fire Station, High Street

Dog and Fox Pub, High Street

Toynbee Fountain, Wimbledon Hill Road

Paul Patisserie, High Street

Nat West Bank, High Street

FROM RIDGWAY TO SOUTH PARK GARDENS

Wimbledon Village Club and Museum

The Wimbledon Village Club and Lecture Hall is situated at the junction of Ridgway and Lingfield Road. It shares the building with the Wimbledon Museum of Local History, and was established in 1858. This Victorian building was designed by Samuel Teulon. The idea of establishing the club championed by local doctor Joseph Toynbee, Thomas Devas and other intellectuals was: "to afford to the inhabitants and more especially the working and middle class of Wimbledon and its vicinity, opportunities of intellectual and moral improvement and rational and social enjoyment through the medium of a reading room, library, lectures and classes." Over the years, members of the club were offered an extensive range of social events and lectures. The building was extended many times to the design of Thomas Jackson. The Wimbledon Museum of Local History is located in the building of the Wimbledon Village Club. The museum shows the history of Wimbledon. Some five thousand objects and over four thousand pictures and photographs show the community's history spanning over three thousand years. This diverse collection portrays Wimbledon's social life in great detail. The collections of the museum are heavily focused on the years of 1850-1980, when Wimbledon started to develop rapidly. Collections include pictures of manor houses from previous centuries, local newspapers and magazines, original documents such as deeds and parish records as well as artefacts like Roman ceramics, Palaeolithic and Neolithic items, and items of clothing and jewellery.

Above: Lecture Hall of Wimbledon
Village Club
Right: Wimbledon Village Club

The Ridgway

The Ridgway is one of the oldest roads in Wimbledon. It was a country lane leading to Kingston and its existence was noted in the Middle Ages. Development came to this road late, in the second part of the nineteenth century with a few Victorian Houses built. Near the High Street end of the road, the Village Club and Emmanuel Church were built and further down the road, Christ Church. Emmanuel Church at 24 Ridgway was built in 1888 according to the Gothic style. This fire-red brick church covered with slates replaced an earlier chapel from 1876 that previously stood here. The church consists of a chancel, a nave, south transept, aisles and west porch. The clock turret houses one bell. The church is evangelical by conviction and was created as a result of a split in the congregation of St Mary's church in 1861. The Swan Pub, previously an inn with the livery stables occupied a prime location on the Ridgway. The stables are still there but instead of carrying passengers to the station in their cabs, the Ridway Stables organise riding lessons and hacking groups on Wimbledon Common. The Swan is a very impressive and popular pub despite boasting some strange phenomena consisting of moving glasses on the tables, attributed to the resident ghost. One ghost however is insignificant compared to the whole bunch of them just round the corner, on the spookiest street in Wimbledon, the Hillside. It is famous for the ghost of a young girl wandering around many gardens in this street in the middle of the night. Another mischievous ghost scatters personal possessions in locked cars. In one of the houses, ink stains appear unexpectedly on the walls and in yet another one, the room traps the residents making an escape impossible. Some suggest that it is the most haunted street because it was here that a spiritualist group engaged in channelling spirits had its headquarters from 1934 to 1941. Probably the most well known medium, Estelle Roberts, conducted many séances and demonstrated many different forms of mediumship including physical materialisation and direct voice. It was here that she supposedly talked to Arthur Conan Doyle amongst many others.

Left:Emmanuel Church, Ridgway
Opposite: The Swan Pub and Ridgway Stables

Edge Hill Road

The steep Edge Hill Road has two interesting buildings, Wimbledon College and the Sacred Heart church. Wimbledon College is a state maintained voluntary aided Roman Catholic Comprehensive Secondary School for boys aged 11 to 18. It is based at Edge Hill and was founded in 1892 by the Jesuits, "for improvement in living and learning to the greatest glory of God and the common good." Before the Jesuits, the school, an imposing building designed by Samuel Teulon, housed from 1860 The Wimbledon School run by headmaster John Brackenbury. That school for boys aged 15 to 18 specialised in preparing pupils for Military Academies. Over the years, many additions changed the original building and sadly, the school Grand Hall burnt down. The Sacred Heart church on the slopes of Edge Hill is a stunning Gothic church opened in 1887. It is a Catholic church which was founded by Edith Arendrup, a member of the wealthy Courtland family. She persuaded the Jesuits from Roehampton to hold mass for the Catholics in a small chapel at her house in Cottenham Park and later on she commissioned Frederick Arthur Walters to design a monumental Gothic church to be built on Edge Hill. The same architect designed yet another Catholic church in Wimbledon, St Winefrid's church at 2 Latimer Road. The Sacred Heart church is of a most complex architecture; the attention to detail is stunning – twin turrets and traceried windows, heavily decorated nave and altars. The building of the church continued for many years; in 1895 the sanctuary and south aisle were finished and a year later, the back chapel. The north aisle and sacristy were opened in 1898, followed by the west front in 1901. Recently, in 2008 the main hall of the church was extended and a massive job of replacing the sunken floor was undertaken. Over one million pounds were spent on this renovation project. The church, despite its huge size, has got a very welcoming presence; it is in the late Decorated Gothic style and is covered with knapped flints. At the entrance there is a highly decorated arch and above, a delicately sculptured window. Inside, the one hundred feet long nave gives the impression of a cathedral rather than a church. The statues of Saints John Berchman, Stanislav Kostka, Francis Borgia, Ignatius, Alphonsus Rodrigues, Peter Clever, Aloysius Gonzaga and Francis Xavier situated above the pillars make the place look grand. Other features worth mentioning are the beautifully carved wooden pulpit, the great Carrara marble Our Lady of Lourdes high altar with reliquary, containing relics of Roman and English martyrs, many interesting stained glass windows, the English martyrs' aisle with some fine statues and finally, the three chapels of St Ignatius, Our Lady and The Sacred Heart.

Wimbledon College, Edge Hill Road

Wimbledon College

A Jesuit school founded in 1892 for improvement in living and learning to the greater glory of God and the common good.

This page and opposite: Sacred Heart
Catholic church on Edge Hill

Christ Church

Christ Church at 16 Copse Hill was built in 1859. It was the second church opened in Wimbledon and it provided services for the rapidly growing local population. The church was designed by Samuel Teulon and built in Kentish rag stone. Within 20 years it proved to be too small, so the south nave was added and the main nave extended. Some of the most interesting features of the interior are the stained glass windows from 1866, the pulpit from 1877, the hammer beam roof and arcading arches in the Decorated style.

Christ Church, Copse Hill
Opposite and overleaf: Holland Gardens

Holland Gardens

Holland Gardens situated on the corner of Pepys Road and Cottenham Park Road were opened in 1929 as a recreation ground. It was a gift to the local community from Lady Holland. Her late husband, Sir Arthur Holland, a head of a successful shipping company was well known for his interest in the local community. He founded Wimbledon Library, was elected the first chairman of the Urban District Council, as well as President of Wimbledon Football Club and was the Borough's second Mayor. The garden is a fitting tribute to the Holland family who dedicated over fifty years to local matters. The gardens, originally a field for grazing cattle, are divided into three areas, the main lawn area with the entrance on Cambridge Road, the second area filled with flowerbeds and some trees and a sports area with twin tennis courts.

THIS LAND WAS GIVEN BY
LADY HOLLAND
OF
HOLMHURST" WIMBLEDON
AND
HER FAMILY.
AS AN OPEN SPACE FOR THE USE AND
ENJOYMENT OF THE PUBLIC, AND WAS NAMED
"HOLLAND GARDENS"
IN COMMEMORATION OF THE BENEFICENT
AND PUBLIC SERVICES OF THE LATE
SIR ARTHUR HOLLAND. J.P.
DURING HIS LONG RESIDENCE IN THE
BOROUGH OF WIMBLEDON

Wimbledon Hill Road and Worple Road

With the opening of the London and South Western Railway in 1838, Wimbledon expanded rapidly and the centre moved to the bottom of Wimbledon Hill. The road was previously known as Bishops Hill and Wimbledon Lane. The most significant building on the street is the Wimbledon Library at number 35. It was designed by Potts, Sulman and Hennings and officially opened on 9 March 1887. Originally, the library consisted of a Reading Room and Lending and Reference Libraries, but within a very short time, due to the library's successful high subscription rate, much larger Lending and Reference Libraries were built at the back of the building. Wimbledon Library has several interesting features on the outside; the walls are decorated with bricks arranged to look like books on shelves and above the highly decorative entrance and balcony, there are Shakespeare and Milton sculptures. The Alexandra pub at number 33 catches the eye with a colourful sign. Inside this old pub, dating from 1876, one can choose to drink in a traditional bar in the front, or in a modern bar at the back of the building. The pub is supposedly haunted by the ghost of a little girl. All the heavy goods from the station and shops had to be transported up the steep hill and as it was difficult for horses, from 1908 until the late 1930s, Jack the trace horse was stationed at the bottom of the Wimbledon Hill assisting heavy vehicles and horse buses to go up the steep incline. Opposite the Alexandra pub, Worple Road starts. Worple Road remained a country lane well into the 1870s. The rapid change came to this part of Wimbledon in the second part of the nineteenth century, when the field between it and the railway line was leased by the All England Croquet Club. Within a few years, the word "tennis" was added into the name of the club and the very first Wimbledon Championship took place in 1877. This new sport drew crowds and the area became popular; new houses were built and the road was extended to Raynes Park. The prominent position on the corner of Worple Road was taken by Ely's

store, previously opened in 1876 by Joseph Ely, on the corner of Broadway and Alexandra Road. It catered for the new suburb's residents and due to growing demand it expanded necessitating the move to the corner of Worple Road. The road was significantly widened between 1905-1907 for trams from Vauxhall to Kingston via Wimbledon and another line from Tooting to Wimbledon.

Library, Wimbledon Hill Road

Above: Library, Wimbledon Hill Road
Opposite: Library wall decoration, Wimbledon Hill Road

MINT VELVET

mintvelvet.co.uk

elys

elys

Above: The Alexandra pub, Wimbledon Hill Road
Left: Elys Department Store, Wimbledon Hill Road

Broadway

Originally a local highway, the Broadway was in the past called New Wimbledon Road or Morden Road. It turned into a busy street with shops and houses in the 1840s to 1870s. As the railway offered the prospect for rapid expansion, by 1900 houses and shops lined almost the entire length of the Broadway. In the year 1905 Wimbledon secured the charter of a town and Alderman Hamshaw became the first Mayor. Council Offices were used temporarily as the Town Hall, but as they were not big enough, in 1930 the foundation stone for the New Town Hall designed by AJ Hope was laid. The new and impressive building of the Town Hall was opened 1931. In 1985 however it became redundant, as Wimbledon was merged into the London Borough of Merton. The current railway station building dates from 1939 and it is the fifth one in less than a hundred years. The first station of 1838 was situated on the opposite side of the road. Trains to London were fast and frequent; for example, in 1909, a train to Waterloo took 14 minutes, and today the same journey takes 17 minutes. New Centre Court Shopping Centre was developed in the 1980s next to Wimbledon Station and incorporated the Town Hall building. A new portico in keeping with the old work was designed by a well known architect, Sir George Grenfell-Baines. The shopping centre boasts two floors of over 60 stores including Debenhams, Gap, M&S, Boots, Whittards and many more. The third floor provides an eating area with cafés and restaurants. Just off Broadway on the side of the Centre Court Shopping Centre there are beautifully preserved façades of the old Magistrates Courts of 1895, Fire Station of 1904, and the highly decorated Baptist Church. A prestigious location on the Broadway is taken by Piazza, a circular pedestrianised area hosting regular markets and performances; it is surrounded by a cluster of shops, restaurants and a cinema. Further down the road all the way to the New Wimbledon Theatre and Polka Theatre there is no shortage of places to stop for a pre-theatre drink or a meal.

Right: Wimbledon Station, Broadway
Opposite: Broadway

Above: Sculpture outside Centre Court
Shopping Centre, Broadway

Left: Old Town Hall, Broadway

Opposite, top left and right: Centre
Court Shopping Centre, Broadway

Opposite, bottom: Broadway outside
Centre Court Shopping Centre

Corner of Broadway and Queen's Road

Old Baptist Church, Queen's Road

Old Magistrates Courts and
Fire Station, Queen's Road

The Piazza, Broadway

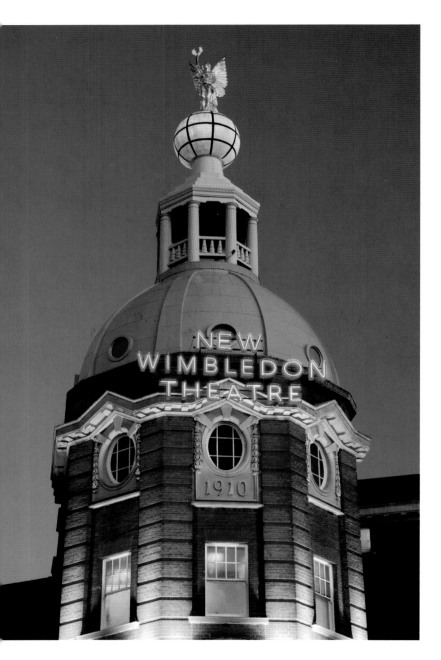

The New Wimbledon Theatre

The New Wimbledon Theatre on the corner of Broadway and Russell Road was opened as "Theatre Royale" on 26 December 1910. This stunning Grade II listed building designed by Cecil Masey and Roy Young was built by J B Mullholland, an actor, theatre lover, play writer and entrepreneur. The theatre quickly gained a glittering reputation as a premier theatrical venue in London. The prominent feature of the theatre visible from afar is the statue of Laetitia, the Roman Goddess of Gaiety atop the dome. It was described in a review in 1910 as follows: The main feature is the tower on the corner, which is surmounted by a dome, above which is a balcony with columns and entablature, which in turn support a crystal ball with a winged figure above. At night the crystal ball will be powerfully illuminated by the mercury vapour process, which throws out violet rays and will be a beacon of light for many miles around" (Mander & Mitchenson's *Theatre of London*). The original capacity of the theatre of 3,000 has been reduced by half but the auditorium decorated in Georgian and Italian Renaissance style has been kept intact. The very first show, the pantomime "Jack and Jill or the Hill, the Well and the Crown" was followed by many successful shows with well known actors like: Gracie Fields, Sybil Thorndike, Ivor Novello and Noel Coward. Despite staging many successful plays, in the 1960s the theatre was threatened with closure. Thanks to strong public support, the local council decided to step in. The theatre was bought from the Mullholland family and refurbished in 1968. From 2003 it has been operating under new management, The Ambassador Theatre Group. The theatre gained the reputation of being a haunted place. There have been numerous sightings of not one, but two ghosts walking through closed doors or levitating through the ceiling. J B Mullholland's ghost supposedly has a habit of sitting in one of the theatre boxes during rehearsals or plays, while a "Grey Lady" prefers to sit in the front row of the gallery. She also mischievously switches on the sprinkler system! Ghosts or no ghosts, the theatre is very much liked and a great success.

Below: The Broadway and New Wimbledon Theatre
Left: Polka Theatre, Broadway
Opposite: Dome of the New Wimbledon Theatre, Broadway

South Park Gardens

South Park Gardens, a registered Grade II landscape on the English Heritage Register of Park and Gardens, is positioned between Dudley Road, Kings Road and Trinity Road. It is a traditional Victorian garden laid out in the late 1800s in a Beaux Arts style derived from the academic teaching of the Ecole des Beaux-Arts in Paris during the nineteenth and early twentieth centuries. The main feature of this style is symmetry in shapes. The park with its scattered trees, serpentine paths, colourful flowerbeds and drinking fountain served local residents well for many years. Deteriorating rapidly in the 1990s, it was restored to its former glory in 2009 thanks to a grant from the Heritage Lottery Fund. The garden is managed by the London Borough of Merton in partnership with Friends of South Park Gardens.

South Park Gardens

South Park Gardens

ANNEX

Wimbledon Map

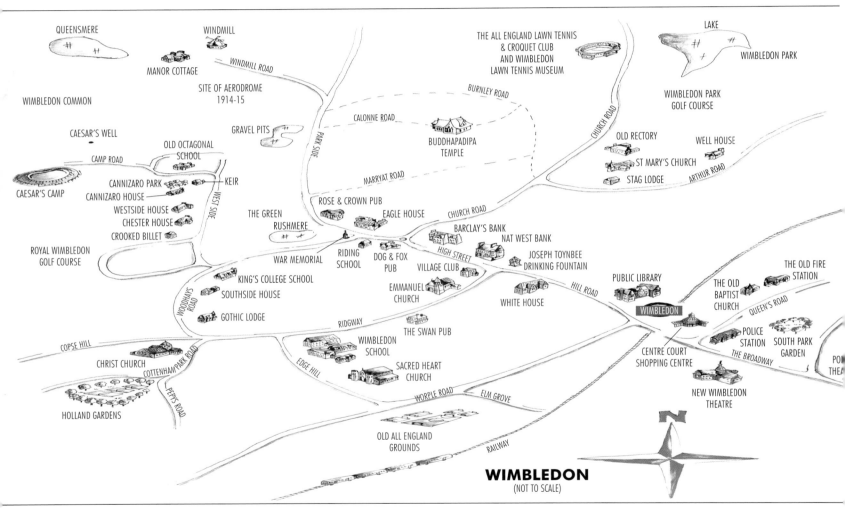

Map drawn by Mariusz Olenkowicz

WIMBLEDON TENNIS PAST WINNERS

Past Men's Single Champions:

1877 S.W. Gore GBR	1913 A.F. Wilding NZL	1959 A.R. Olmedo USA
1878 P.F. Hadow GBR	1914 N.E. Brookes AUS	1960 N.A. Fraser AUS
1879 J.T. Hartley GBR	1919 G.L. Patterson AUS	1961 R.G. Laver AUS
1880 J.T. Hartley GBR	1920 W.T. Tilden USA	1962 R.G. Laver AUS
1881 W.C. Renshaw GBR	1921 W.T. Tilden USA	1963 C.R. McKinley USA
1882 W.C. Renshaw GBR	1922 G.L. Patterson AUS	1964 R.S. Emerson AUS
1883 W.C. Renshaw GBR	1923 W. M. Johnston USA	1965 R.S. Emerson AUS
1884 W.C. Renshaw GBR	1924 J.R. Borotra FRA	1966 M.M. Santana ESP
1885 W.C. Renshaw GBR	1925 J.R. Lacoste FRA	1967 J.D. Newcombe AUS
1886 W.C. Renshaw GBR	1926 J.R. Borotra FRA	1968 R.G. Laver AUS
1887 H.F. Lawford GBR	1927 H.J. Cochet FRA	1969 R.G. Laver AUS
1888 J.E. Renshaw GBR	1928 J.R. Lacoste FRA	1970 J.D. Newcombe AUS
1889 W.C. Renshaw GBR	1929 H.J. Cochet FRA	1971 J.D. Newcombe AUS
1890 W.J. Hamilton GBR	1930 W.T. Tilden USA	1972 S.R. Smith USA
1891 W. Baddeley GBR	1931 S.B.B. Wood USA	1973 J. Kodes TCH
1892 W. Baddeley GBR	1932 H.E.Vines USA	1974 J.S. Connors USA
1893 J. Pim GBR	1933 J.H. Crawford AUS	1975 A.R. Ashe USA
1894 J. Pim GBR	1934 F.J. Perry GBR	1976 B.R. Borg SWE
1895 W. Baddeley GBR	1935 F.J. Perry GBR	1977 B.R. Borg SWE
1896 H.S. Mahony GBR	1936 F.J. Perry GBR	1978 B.R. Borg SWE
1897 R.F. Doherty GBR	1937 J.D. Budge USA	1979 B.R. Borg SWE
1898 R.F. Doherty GBR	1938 J.D. Budge USA	1980 B.R. Borg SWE
1899 R.F. Doherty GBR	1939 R.L. Riggs USA	1981 J.P. McEnroe USA
1900 R.F. Doherty GBR	1946 Y.F.M. Petra FRA	1982 J.S. Connors USA
1901 A.W. Gore GBR	1947 J.A. Kramer USA	1983 J.P. McEnroe USA
1902 H.L. Doherty GBR	1948 R. Falkenburg USA	1984 J.P. McEnroe USA
1903 H.L. Doherty GBR	1949 F.R. Schroeder USA	1985 B.F. Becker GER
1904 H.L. Doherty GBR	1950 J.E. Patty USA	1986 B.F. Becker GER
1905 H.L. Doherty GBR	1951 R. Savitt USA	1987 P.H. Cash AUS
1906 H.L. Doherty GBR	1952 F.A. Sedgman AUS	1988 S.B. Edberg SWE
1907 N.E. Brookes AUS	1953 E.V. Seixas USA	1989 B.F. Becker GER
1908 A.W. Gore GBR	1954 J. Drobny EGY	1990 S.B. Edberg SWE
1909 A.W. Gore GBR	1955 M.A. Trabert USA	1991 M.D. Stich GER
1910 A.F. Wilding NZL	1956 L.A. Hoad AUS	1992 A.K. Agassi USA
1911 A.F. Wilding NZL	1957 L.A. Hoad AUS	1993 P. Sampras USA
1912 A.F. Wilding NZL	1958 A.J. Cooper AUS	1994 P. Sampras USA

1995 P. Sampras USA
1996 R.P.S. Krajicek NED
1997 P. Sampras USA
1998 P. Sampras USA
1999 P. Sampras USA
2000 P. Sampras USA
2001 G.S. Ivanisevic CRO
2002 L.G. Hewitt AUS
2003 R. Federer SUI
2004 R. Federer SUI
2005 R. Federer SUI
2006 R. Federer SUI
2007 R. Federer SUI
2008 R. Nadal ESP
2009 R. Federer SUI
2010 R. Nadal ESP

Past Women's Singles Champions

1884 Miss M.E.E. Watson GBR
1885 Miss M.E.E. Watson GBR
1886 Miss B. Bingley GBR
1887 Miss C. Dod GBR
1888 Miss C. Dod GBR
1889 Mrs. G.W. Hillyard GBR
1890 Miss H.G.B. Rice GBR
1891 Miss C. Dod GBR
1892 Miss C. Dod GBR
1893 Miss C. Dod GBR
1894 Mrs. G.W. Hillyard GBR
1895 Miss C.R. Cooper GBR
1896 Miss C.R. Cooper GBR
1897 Mrs. G.W. Hillyard GBR
1898 Miss C.R. Cooper GBR
1899 Mrs. G.W. Hillyard GBR
1900 Mrs. G.W. Hillyard GBR
1901 Mrs. A. Sterry GBR
1902 Miss M.E. Robb GBR
1903 Miss D.K. Douglass GBR
1904 Miss D.K. Douglass GBR
1905 Miss M.G. Sutton USA
1906 Miss D.K. Douglass GBR

1907 Miss M.G. Sutton USA
1908 Mrs. A. Sterry GBR
1909 Miss P.D.H. Boothby GBR
1910 Mrs. R.L. Chambers GBR
1911 Mrs. R.L. Chambers GBR
1912 Mrs. D.T.R. Larcombe GBR
1913 Mrs. R.L. Chambers GBR
1914 Mrs. R.L. Chambers GBR
1919 Miss S.R.F. Lenglen FRA
1920 Miss S.R.F. Lenglen FRA
1921 Miss S.R.F. Lenglen FRA
1922 Miss S.R.F. Lenglen FRA
1923 Miss S.R.F. Lenglen FRA
1924 Miss K. McKane GBR
1925 Miss S.R.F. Lenglen FRA
1926 Mrs. L.A. Godfree GBR
1927 Miss H.N. Wills USA
1928 Miss H.N. Wills USA
1929 Miss H.N. Wills USA
1930 Mrs. F.S. Moody USA
1931 Miss C. Aussem GER
1932 Mrs. F.S. Moody USA
1933 Mrs. F.S. Moody USA
1934 Miss D.E. Round GBR
1935 Mrs. F.S. Moody USA
1936 Miss H.H. Jacobs USA
1937 Miss D.E. Round GBR
1938 Mrs. F.S. Moody USA
1939 Miss A. Marble USA
1946 Miss P.M. Betz USA
1947 Miss M.E. Osborne USA
1948 Miss A.L. Brough USA
1949 Miss A.L. Brough USA
1950 Miss A.L. Brough USA
1951 Miss D.J. Hart USA
1952 Miss M.C. Connolly USA — '67
1953 Miss M.C. Connolly USA
1954 Miss M.C. Connolly USA
1955 Miss A.L. Brough USA
1956 Miss S.J. Fry USA
1957 Miss A. Gibson USA
1958 Miss A. Gibson USA

1959 Miss M.E.A. Bueno BRA
1960 Miss M.E.A. Bueno BRA
1961 Miss F.A.M. Mortimer GBR
1962 Mrs J.R. Susman USA
1963 Miss M. Smith AUS
1964 Miss M.E.A. Bueno BRA DIED 6/18
1965 Miss M. Smith AUS
1966 Mrs L.W. King USA
1967 Mrs L.W. King USA
1968 Mrs L.W. King USA
1969 Mrs P.F. Jones GBR
1970 Mrs B.M. Court AUS
1971 Miss E.F. Goolagong AUS
1972 Mrs L.W. King USA
1973 Mrs L.W. King USA
1974 Miss C.M. Evert USA
1975 Mrs L.W. King USA
1976 Miss C.M. Evert USA
1977 Miss S.V. Wade GBR
1978 Miss M. Navratilova USA
1979 Miss M. Navratilova USA
1980 Mrs R.A. Cawley AUS
1981 Mrs J.M. Lloyd USA
1982 Miss M. Navratilova USA
1983 Miss M. Navratilova USA
1984 Miss M. Navratilova USA
1985 Miss M. Navratilova USA
1986 Miss M. Navratilova USA
1987 Miss M. Navratilova USA
1988 Miss S.M. Graf GER
1989 Miss S.M. Graf GER
1990 Miss M. Navratilova USA
1991 Miss S.M. Graf GER
1992 Miss S.M. Graf GER
1993 Miss S.M. Graf GER
1994 Miss I.C. Martinez ESP
1995 Miss S.M. Graf GER
1996 Miss S.M. Graf GER
1997 Miss M. Hingis SUI
1998 Miss J. Novotna CZE
1999 Miss L.A. Davenport USA
2000 Miss V.E.S. Williams USA

2001 Miss V.E.S. Williams USA
2002 Miss S.J. Williams USA
2003 Miss S.J. Williams USA
2004 Miss M. Sharapova RUS
2005 Miss V.E.S. Williams USA
2006 Miss A. Mauresmo FRA
2007 Miss V.E.S. Williams USA
2008 Miss V.E.S. Williams USA
2009 Miss S.J. Williams USA
2010 Miss S.J. Williams USA

Men's Doubles Champions

1884 J.E. Renshaw and W.C. Renshaw GBR
1885 J.E. Renshaw and W.C. Renshaw GBR
1886 J.E. Renshaw and W.C. Renshaw GBR
1887 P. Bowes-Lyon and H.W.W. Wilberforce GBR
1888 J.E. Renshaw and W.C. Renshaw GBR
1889 J.E. Renshaw and W.C. Renshaw GBR
1890 J. Pim and F.O. Stoker GBR
1891 H. Baddeley and W. Baddeley GBR
1892 H. S. Barlow and E. W. Lewis GBR
1893 J. Pim and F.O. Stoker GBR
1894 W. Baddelely and H. Baddeley GBR
1895 H. Baddeley and W. Baddeley GBR
1896 H. Baddeley and W. Baddeley GBR
1897 H.L. Doherty and R.F. Doherty GBR
1898 H.L. Doherty and R.F. Doherty GBR
1899 H.L. Doherty and R.F. Doherty GBR
1900 H.L. Doherty and R.F. Doherty GBR
1901 H.L. Doherty and R.F. Doherty GBR
1902 F.L. Riseley and S.H. Smith GBR
1903 H.L. Doherty and R.F. Doherty GBR
1904 H.L. Doherty and R.F. Doherty GBR
1905 H.L. Doherty and R.F. Doherty GBR
1906 F.L. Riseley and S.H. Smith GBR
1907 N.E. Brooks AUS and A.F. Wilding NZL
1908 M.J.G. Ritchie GBR and A.F. Wilding NZL
1909 H.R. Barratt and A.W. Gore GBR
1910 M.J.G. Ritchie GBR and A.F. Wilding NZL
1911 M.O. Decugis and A.H. Gobert FRA
1912 H.R. Barratt and C.P. Dixon GBR
1913 H.R. Barratt and C.P. Dixon GBR
1914 N.E. Brookes AUS and A.F.Wilding NZL
1919 R.V. Thomas and P. O'Hara-Wood AUS
1920 C. S. Garland and R.N. Williams USA
1921 R. Lycett and M. Woosnam GBR
1922 J.O. Anderson AUS and R. Lycett GBR
1923 R. Lycett and L.A. Godfree GBR
1924 F. T. Hunter and V. Richards USA
1925 J.R. Borotra and J.R. Lacoste FRA
1926 J. Brugnon and H.J. Cochet FRA
1927 F. T. Hunter and W. T. Tilden USA
1928 J. Brugnon and H.J. Cochet FRA
1929 W.L. Allison and J.W. Van Ryn USA
1930 W.L. Allison and J.W. Van Ryn USA
1931 G. M. Lott and J.W. Van Ryn USA
1932 J.R. Borotra and J. Brugnon FRA
1933 J.R. Borotra and J. Brugnon FRA
1934 G. M. Lott and L.R. Stoefen USA
1935 J. H. Crawford and A.K. Quist AUS
1936 G. P. Hughes and C.R.D. Tuckey GBR
1937 J.D.Budge and C.G. Mako USA
1938 J.D. Budge and C.G. Mako USA
1939 R. L. Riggs and E.T. Cooke USA
1946 T.P. Brown and J.A. Kramer USA
1947 R. Falkenburg and J.A. Kramer USA
1948 J.E. Bromwich and F.A. Sedgman AUS
1949 R.A. Gonzales and F.A. Parker USA
1950 J.E. Bromwich and A.K. Quist AUS
1951 K.B. McGregor and F.A. Sedgman AUS
1952 K.B. McGregor and F.A. Sedgman AUS
1953 L.A. Hoad and K.R. Rosewall AUS
1954 R.N. Hartwig and M.G. Rose AUS
1955 R.N. Hartwig and L.A. Hoad AUS
1956 L.A. Hoad and K.R. Rosewall AUS
1957 G.P. Mulloy and J.E. Patty USA
1958 S.V. Davidson and U.C.J. Schmidt SWE
1959 R.S. Emerson and N.A. Fraser AUS
1960 R.H. Osuna MEX and R.D. Ralston USA
1961 R.S. Emerson and N.A. Fraser AUS
1962 R.A.J. Hewitt and F.S. Stolle AUS
1963 R.H. Osuna and A. Palafox MEX
1964 R.A.J. Hewitt and F.S. Stolle AUS
1965 J.D. Newcombe and A.D. Roche AUS
1966 K.N. Fletcher and J.D. Newcombe AUS
1967 R.A.J. Hewitt and F.D. McMillan RSA
1968 J.D. Newcombe and A.D. Roche AUS
1969 J.D. Newcombe and A.D. Roche AUS
1970 J.D. Newcombe and A.D. Roche AUS
1971 R.S. Emerson and R.G. Laver AUS
1972 R.A.J. Hewitt and F.D. McMillan RSA
1973 J.S. Connors USA and I. Nastase ROM
1974 J.D. Newcombe and A.D. Roche AUS
1975 V. Gerulaitis and A.A. Mayer USA
1976 B.E. Gottfried USA and R.C. Ramirez MEX
1977 R.L. Case and G. Masters AUS
1978 R.A.J. Hewitt and F.D. McMillan RSA
1979 P.B. Fleming and J.P. McEnroe USA

1980 P.B. McNamara and P.F. McNamee AUS
1981 P.B. Fleming and J.P. McEnroe USA
1982 P.B. McNamara and P.F. McNamee AUS
1983 P.B. Fleming and J.P. McEnroe USA
1984 P.B. Fleming and J.P. McEnroe USA
1985 H.P. Guenthardt SUI and B. Taroczy HUN
1986 J.K. Nystrom and M.A.O. Wilander SWE
1987 K.E. Flach and R.A. Seguso USA
1988 K.E. Flach and R.A. Seguso USA
1989 J.B. Fitzgerald AUS and A. Jarryd SWE
1990 R.D. Leach and J.R. Pugh USA
1991 J.B. Fitzgerald AUS and A.P. Jarryd SWE
1992 J.P. McEnroe USA and M.D. Stich GER
1993 T.A. Woodbridge and M.R. Woodforde AUS
1994 T.A. Woodbridge and M.R. Woodforde AUS
1995 T.A. Woodbridge and M.R. Woodforde AUS
1996 T.A. Woodbridge and M.R. Woodforde AUS
1997 T.A. Woodbridge and M.R. Woodforde AUS
1998 J.F. Eltingh and P.V.N. Haarhuis NED
1999 M.S. Bhupathi and L.A. Paes IND
2000 T.A. Woodbridge and M.R. Woodforde AUS
2001 D.J. Johnson and J.E. Palmer USA
2002 J.L. Bjorkman SWE and T.A. Woodbridge AUS
2003 J.L. Bjorkman SWE and T.A. Woodbridge AUS
2004 J.L. Bjorkman SWE and T.A. Woodbridge AUS

2005 S. Huss AUS and W. Moodie RSA
2006 B. Bryan and M. Bryan USA
2007 A. Clement and M. Llodra FRA
2008 D. Nestor CAN and N. Zimonjic SRB
2009 D. Nestor CAN and N. Zimonjic SRB
2010 J. Melzer AUT and P. Petzschner GER

Women's Doubles Champions

1913 R.J. McNair GBR and P.D.H. Boothby GBR
1914 E.M. Ryan USA and A.M. Morton GBR
1919 S.R.F. Lenglen FRA and E.M. Ryan USA
1920 S.R.F. Lenglen FRA and E.M. Ryan USA
1921 S.R.F. Lenglen FRA and E.M. Ryan USA
1922 S.R.F. Lenglen FRA and E.M. Ryan USA
1923 S.R.F. Lenglen FRA and E.M. Ryan USA
1924 G. Wightman USA and H.N. Wills USA
1925 S.R.F. Lenglen FRA and E.M. Ryan USA
1926 E.M. Ryan USA and M.K. Browne USA
1927 H.N. Wills USA and E.M. Ryan USA
1928 M.R. Watson and M.A. Saunders GBR
1929 M.R. Watson and L.R.C. Michell
1930 F.S. Moody USA and E.M. Ryan USA
1931 W.P. Barron GBR and P.E. Mudford GBR
1932 D.E. Metaxa FRA and J. Sigart BEL
1933 R. Mathieu FRA and E.M. Ryan USA

1934 R. Mathieu FRA and E.M. Ryan USA
1935 W.A. James GBR and K.E. Stammers GBR
1936 W.A. James GBR and K.E. Stammers GBR
1937 R. Mathieu FRA and A.M. Yorke GBR
1938 M. Fabyan USA and A. Marble USA
1939 M. Fabyan USA and A. Marble USA
1946 A.L. Brough USA and M.E. Osborne USA
1947 D.J. Hart USA and R.B. Todd USA
1948 A.L. Brough USA and W. du Pont USA
1949 A.L. Brough USA and W. du Pont USA
1950 A.L. Brough USA and W. du Pont USA
1951 S.J. Fry USA and D.J. Hart USA
1952 S.J. Fry USA and D.J. Hart USA
1953 S.J. Fry USA and D.J. Hart USA
1954 A.L. Brough USA and W. du Pont USA
1955 F.A.M. Mortimer and J.A. Shilcock GBR
1956 A. Buxton GBR and A. Gibson USA
1957 A. Gibson USA and D.R. Hard USA
1958 M.E.A. Bueno BRA and A. Gibson USA
1959 J.M. Arth USA and D.R. Hard USA
1960 M.E.A. Bueno BRA and D.R. Hard USA
1961 K.J. Hantze USA and B.J. Moffitt USA
1962 B.J. Moffitt USA and J.R. Susman USA
1963 M.E.A. Bueno BRA and D.R. Hard USA
1964 M. Smith AUS and L.R. Turner AUS
1965 M.E.A. Bueno BRA and B.J. Moffitt USA
1966 M.E.A. Bueno BRA and N.A. Richey

USA
1967 R. Casals USA and L.W. King USA
1968 R. Casals USA and L.W. King USA
1969 B.M. Court AUS and J.A.M. Tegart AUS
1970 R. Casals USA and Mrs L.W. King USA
1971 R. Casals USA and Mrs L.W. King USA
1972 L.W. King USA and B.F. Stove NED
1973 R. Casals USA and L.W. King USA
1974 E.F. Goolagong AUS and M.S.A. Michel USA
1975 A.K. Kiyomura USA and K. Sawamatsu JAP
1976 C.M. Evert USA and M. Navratilova TCH
1977 R.L. Cawley AUS and J.C. Russell USA
1978 G.E. Reid AUS and W.M. Turnbull AUS
1979 L.W. King USA and M. Navratilova USA
1980 K. Jordan USA and A.E. Smith USA
1981 M. Navratilova USA and P.H. Shriver USA
1982 M. Navratilova USA and P.H. Shriver USA
1983 M. Navratilova USA and P.H. Shriver USA
1984 M. Navratilova USA and P.H. Shriver USA
1985 K. Jordan USA and P D. Smylie AUS
1986 M. Navratilova USA and P.H. Shriver USA
1987 C.G. Kohde-Kilsh GER and H. Sukova TCH
1988 S.M. Graf GER and G.B. Sabatini ARG
1989 J. Novotna TCH and H. Sukova TCH

1990 J. Novotna TCH and H. Sukova TCH
1991 L.I. Savchenko and N.M. Zvereva URS
1992 B.C. Fernandez USA and N.M. Zvereva CIS
1993 B.C. Fernandez USA and N.M. Zvereva BLR
1994 B.C. Fernandez USA and N.M. Zvereva BLR
1995 J. Novotna CZE and A.I.M. Sanchez-Vicario ESP
1996 M. Hingis SUI and H. Sukova CZE
1997 B.C. Fernandez USA and N.M. Zvereva BLR
1998 M. Hingis SUI and J. Novotna CZE
1999 L.A. Davenport USA and C.M. Morariu USA
2000 V.E.S. Williams USA and S.J. Williams USA
2001 L.M. RaymondUSA and R.P. Stubbs AUS
2002 V.E.S. Williams USA and S.J. Williams USA
2003 K. Clijsters BEL and A. Sugiyama JPN
2004 C. Black ZIM and R. Stubbs AUS
2005 C. Black ZIM and L. Huber RSA
2006 Y. Yan CHN and J. Zheng CHN
2007 C. Black ZIM and L. Huber RSA
2008 V.E.S. Williams USA and S.J. Williams USA
2009 V.E.S. Williams USA and S.J. Williams USA
2010 V. King USA and Y. Shvedova KAZ

Mixed Doubles Champions

1913 H. Crisp and C.O. Tuckey GBR
1914 J.C. Parke and D.T.R. Larcombe GBR
1919 R. Lycett GBR and E.M. Ryan USA

1920 G. L. Patterson AUS and S.R.F. Lenglen FRA
1921 R. Lycett GBR and E.M. Ryan USA
1922 P.O. Wood AUS and S.R.F. Lenglen FRA
1923 R. Lycett GBR and E.M. Ryan USA
1924 J.B. Gilbert and K. McKane GBR
1925 J.R. Borotra and S.R.F. Lenglen FRA
1926 L.A. Godfree and L.A. Godfree GBR
1927 F.T. Hunter and E.M. Ryan USA
1928 P.D.B. Spence RSA and E.M Ryan USA
1929 F.T. Hunter and H.N. Wills USA
1930 J.H. Crawford AUS and E.M Ryan USA
1931 G.M. Lott and L.A. Harper USA
1932 E.G. Maier and E.M Ryan USA
1933 G. von Cramm and H. Krahwinkel GER
1934 R. Miki JPN and D.E. Round GBR
1935 F.J. Perry and D.E. Round GBR
1936 F.J. Perry and D.E. Round GBR
1937 J.D. Budge and A. Marble USA
1938 J.D. Budge and A. Marble USA
1939 R.L. Riggs and A. Marble USA
1946 T.P. Brown and A.L. Brough USA
1947 J.E. Bromwich AUS and A.L. Brough USA
1948 J.E. Bromwich AUS and A.L. Brough USA
1949 E.W. Sturgess and R.A. Summers RSA
1950 E.W. Sturgess RSA and A.L. Brough USA
1951 F.A. Sedgman AUS and D.J. Hart USA
1952 F.A. Sedgman AUS and D.J. Hart USA
1953 E.V. Seixas and D.J. Hart USA
1954 E.V. Seixas and D.J. Hart USA
1955 E.V. Seixas and D.J. Hart USA

1956 E.V. Seixas and S.J. Fry USA
1957 M.G. Rose AUS and D.R. Hard USA
1958 R.N. Howe and L.G. Coghlan AUS
1959 R.G. Laver AUS and D.R. Hard USA
1960 R.G. Laver AUS and D.R. Hard USA
1961 F.S. Stolle and L.R. Turner AUS
1962 N.A. Fraser AUS and W. du Pont USA
1963 K.N. Fletcher and M. Smith AUS
1964 F.S. Stolle and L.R. Turner AUS
1965 K.N. Fletcher and M. Smith AUS
1966 K.N. Fletcher and M. Smith AUS
1967 O.K. Davidson AUS and L.W. King USA
1968 K.N. Fletcher and B.M. Court AUS
1969 F.S. Stolle AUS and P.F. Jones GBR
1970 I. Nastase ROM and R. Casals USA
1971 O.K. Davidson AUS and L.W. King USA
1972 I. Nastase ROM and R. Casals USA
1973 O.K. Davidson AUS and L.W. King USA
1974 O.K. Davidson AUS and L.W. King USA
1975 M.C. Riessen USA and B.M. Court AUS

1976 A.D. Roche AUS and F.G. Durr FRA
1977 R.A.J. Hewitt and G.R. Stevens RSA
1978 F.D. McMillan RSA and B.F. Stove NED
1979 R.A.J. Hewitt and G.R. Stevens RSA
1980 J.R. Austin and T.A. Austin USA
1981 F.D. McMillan RSA and B.F. Stove NED
1982 K.M. Curren RSA and A.E. Smith USA
1983 J.M. Lloyd GBR and W.M. Turnbull AUS
1984 J.M. Lloyd GBR and W.M. Turnbull AUS
1985 P.F. McNamee AUS and M. Navratilova USA
1986 K.E. Flach and K. Jordan USA
1987 M.J. Bates and J.M. Durie GBR
1988 S.E. Stewart and Z.L. Garrison USA
1989 J.R. Pugh USA and J. Novotna TCH
1990 R.D. Leach and Z.L. Garrison USA
1991 J.B. Fitzgerald and P.D. Smylie AUS
1992 C. Suk TCH and A. Neiland LAT
1993 M.R. Woodforde AUS and M. Navratilova USA
1994 T.A. Woodbridge AUS and H. Sukova CZE

1995 J.A. Stark and M. Navratilova USA
1996 C. Suk and H. Sukova CZE
1997 C. Suk and H. Sukova CZE
1998 M.N. Mirnyi BLR and S.J. Williams USA
1999 L.A. Paes IND and L.M. Raymond USA
2000 D.J. Johnson and K.Y. Po USA
2001 L Friedl CZE and D. Hantuchova SVK
2002 M Bhupathi IND and E. Likhovteva RUS
2003 L.A. Paes IND and M. Navratilova USA
2004 W.H. Black ZIM and C.C. Black ZIM
2005 M. Bhupathi IND and M. Pierce FRA
2006 A. Ram ISR and V. Zvonareva RUS
2007 J. Murray GBR and J. Jankovic SRB
2008 B. Bryan USA and S. Stosur AUS
2009 M. Knowles BAH and A. Groenefeld GER
2010 L.A. Paes IND and C.C. Black ZIM